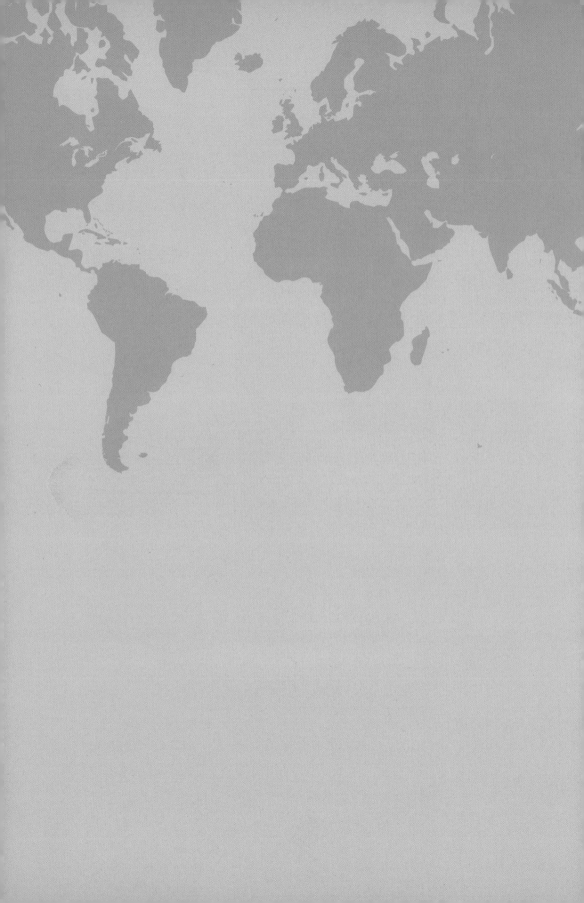

GLOBAL INDUSTRIES
UNCOVERED

THE SPORTS INDUSTRY

EWAN MCLEISH

WAYLAND

First published in 2009 by Wayland

Copyright © Wayland 2009

Wayland
338 Euston Road
London NW1 3BH

Wayland Australia
Level 17/207 Kent Street
Sydney NSW 2000

Senior Editor: Claire Shanahan
Consultant: Steph Warren
Designer: Rebecca Painter
Picture Researcher: Shelley Noronha

British Library Cataloguing in Publication Data
 McLeish, Ewan.
   The sports industry. -- (Global industries uncovered)
   1. Sports--Economic aspects--Juvenile literature.
   2. Sports- -Marketing--Juvenile literature.
   3. Industrial location-- Juvenile literature.
   4. Globalization--Economic aspects--
Juvenile literature.
   I. Title II. Series
   338.4'7796-dc22
ISBN 978 0 7502 5825 8

Picture acknowledgements:
Cover and page 36 © Ben Radford/Corbis; 6 Nelson
Mandela Getty Images; 9 Getty Images Sport; 11
Getty Images; 12 India AFP/Getty Images; 14
WireImage/ Getty Images; 15 © Stefan
Zaklin/epa/Corbis; 16, 17, 21, 32 Rex Features Ltd; 19,
30, 37 Getty Images; 20 Popperfoto/Getty Images; 23,
34, 35, 39 AFP/Getty Images; 24 © Olivier Prevosto/
TempSport/Corbis; 26 Bongarts/Getty Images; 28 ©
Sean Masterson/epa/Corbis; 29 © Elisa Haberer
/Corbis; 33 © Schlegelmilch/Corbis; 41 Players Dr. Liz
Odera/Professional Tennis Registry/
http://www.globalgiving.com
http://www.tennisafrica.info/

Printed in Malaysia

Wayland is a division of Hachette Children's Books, an
Hachette UK company.
www.hachette.co.uk

Contents

CASE STUDIES
UNCOVERED

A global industry

Faisal lives in Dubai in the Middle East. He is 13 years old and a Manchester United fan. He has never been to England but he watches all their matches on satellite TV. When he is not at school, he wears a Man U shirt with the number of his favourite player on the back. He is one of 75 million such fans worldwide. Although he does not know it, Faisal is part of a global industry worth billions of pounds. That global industry is sport.

We live in a world in which sport plays an increasingly important role. Some of the world's most dramatic (and most widely viewed) international events are related to sporting competitions or matches. When Italy won the World Cup in 2006, the event was seen on television by an estimated 260 million viewers. Politicians and world leaders increasingly want to be associated with sport. When South Africa won the Rugby World Cup in 1995, the country's new leader, Nelson Mandela, was seen wearing the famous Springbok jersey as he presented the cup to the winning captain.

The importance of international sport can be seen in this picture as the winning Rugby World Cup captain, Francois Pienaar, shakes hands with South Africa's then President, Nelson Mandela, in 1995.

Going global

So what exactly do we mean by the term 'globalisation' and what are global industries? Global industries work across different nations and continents to create, and usually sell, their products and services on a worldwide basis. They contribute to what is known as 'the global economy'; that is, they have a significant impact on the way revenue, or income, is generated around the world.

SPOTLIGHT

Globalisation: a shrinking world

Globalisation means that we live in a smaller, more connected, more interdependent world. Of course, physically, the world is not smaller, but it feels that way because it is more accessible. Geographical distances seem reduced because it takes less time to travel or communicate between them. This has been made mainly possible by improvements in technology. Mobile phones, the internet, low-cost flights and cheaper cars are all examples of this. Global connections are faster, easier and cheaper, so industries use them more. We tend to take this for granted, but the technological revolution has not taken place at the same rate all over the world. As a result, some countries have benefited more than others from globalisation.

Globalisation also means that the boundaries between countries themselves become less distinct. For example, countries belonging to the European Union (EU) have combined some of their powers, economic transactions and decision-making processes under a European Parliament and a Council of Ministers.

Globalisation of sport

In terms of sport, the main characteristics of globalisation are economic but there also have other implications. For example, while many sports are booming in large cities, where there is the finance and other infrastructure to support them, the development of sport in regional or poorer areas is declining. Globalisation in sport can be seen in the increase in the number of powerful international sporting bodies and agencies, such as the International Olympic Committee (IOC) and Fédération Internationale de Football Association (FIFA), the transfer of sports finance across national and international boundaries, and the way in which global communications can bring a single sporting event to a global audience.

A big industry

Today, sport, in all its forms, makes a major contribution to the global economy. In fact, many people now consider it to be the largest single employer in the world. As well as attracting the largest audiences of any activity on the planet, it has produced many of the best-known celebrities, such as David Beckham and Maria Sharapova, and the biggest global brands, such as Nike and Adidas. A single player,such as the US golfer Tiger Woods, can earn up to US$100 million a year from prize money and endorsements (attaching a player's name to a particular product or brand). Sport commands the highest-value TV and communications contracts. The international movement of supporters and spectators to different events is now vital to the travel and tourist industry. Sporting goods industries alone are estimated to have an annual retail market of £400 billion – more than the total yearly income of many countries.

SPOTLIGHT

Golfonomics

In the USA alone, golf generates an annual US$76 billion. This means it outstrips the film and music industries as well as all other major spectator sports combined. About 2 million people are employed directly in the game, working at 16,000 golf courses and driving ranges, or in related industries such as golf wear- and golf club-manufacture. Each year, Americans spend US$6.2 billion on golf-related products and another US$860 million on golfing magazines. When the 'multiplier effect' on other industries such as tourism, land (real estate) and the media is taken into account, the overall figure rockets to US$165 billion a year. In the European zone, which in golfing terms now includes Africa and the Middle East, the golfing industry is now worth US$42 billion per year and is growing.

This table shows the clubs with the highest estimated economic value (figures are in millions of dollars). Overall, the table is dominated by American football, although soccer leads the table with the English club Manchester United (see Case Study on pages 20-25).

Club	Sport	Value (US$ millions)
Manchester United	Football	1800
Dallas Cowboys	American football	1612
Washington Redskins	American football	1538
New England Patriots	American football	1324
New York Yankees	Baseball	1306
Real Madrid	Football	1285
Arsenal	Football	1200
New York Giants	American football	1178
New York Jets	American football	1170
Houston Texans	American football	1125

A wider importance

Sport is not just economically important. It also plays a unique role in connecting people through a common interest. This often goes beyond geographical, cultural, racial or even religious interests. Almost every government around the world puts funding into sporting infrastructure, for example sporting venues and community sport initiatives. They recognise the benefits that sport can bring, for example, in terms of fitness and health, education, community development, job creation and the prevention of crime. They also appreciate the role sport plays in establishing ideas of national identity and pride. In short, they recognise that sport matters to people.

Young sports stars, like the British Olympic diver, Tom Daley, are already well known around the world. Here Tom Daley signs autographs for fans during the Olympic and Paralympic Heroes Parade in October 2008.

SPOTLIGHT

Sport – a force for good?

There is much evidence to suggest that community-based sports programmes can reduce levels of street crime. In Kansas City, USA, evening and midnight basketball programmes reduced the crime rate among young men by nearly 50 per cent. There was also a reduction in crime among young women who took part in a running programme in Alexandria in Virginia, USA. In Australia, schemes that engaged young offenders in organised sport significantly reduced re-offending rates. In the UK, a scheme called 'Splash Extra', involving 91,000 young people in sporting and art-related activities, accounted for a 31 per cent reduction in street crime. Such schemes are only successful, however, when they are maintained. In 2007, the United Nations (UN) established a 'Global Sport Fund' to 'engage youth from different parts of the world, particularly those from conflict regions, in sport. The aim is to promote sports activity among young people and to prevent drug use and crime.

> *The hidden face of sport is the tens of thousands who find, in their football, rowing, athletics or rock climbing clubs, a place for meetings and exchange, but, above all, the training ground for community life....[Here] people learn to take responsibility, to follow rules, to accept one another, to look for consensus [agreement], to take on democracy.*

Daniel Tarschys, Secretary General
of the Council of Europe, 1995

What is a global sport?

What makes a particular sport global? It is hard to find one sport that is universally popular. Even the most powerful nation in the world, the USA, has been only partially successful in 'exporting' American games to other parts of the world. Baseball, for example, has only really become established outside the USA in parts of the Caribbean and countries such as Japan and South Korea. Basketball and volleyball have been more successful internationally and ice hockey is now popular in many parts of Europe. The world's most popular sport, football (or soccer, as Americans refer to it), on the other hand, is not as important inside the USA as many other games. One question we need to ask, therefore, is 'what do we mean by most popular or most global?' This could refer to 'most watched or supported', 'most played' or 'most revenue generating'. In terms of 'most watched', the following sports are most frequently mentioned in top ten lists.

Sport	Fan base		Where principally followed
Football (soccer)	3.3–3.5	billion	Europe, Africa, Asia, Americas
Cricket	2.3	billion	India, UK, Pakistan, Asia, Australia
Field Hockey	2–2.2	billion	Asia, Europe, Africa, Australia
Tennis	1.0	billion	Europe, Americas, Asia
Volleyball	900	million	Asia, Europe, Americas, Australia
Table tennis	900	million	Asia, Europe, Africa, Americas
Baseball	500	million	USA, Japan, Cuba, Dominican Republic
Golf	400	million	USA, Canada, Europe
American football (NLF)	390–410	million	USA mainly
Basketball	400	million	USA, Canada mainly

This table shows the estimated number of followers of the ten most popular sports. Volleyball is probably the most widely played game in the world although it receives little media coverage. Perhaps surprisingly, athletics does not appear in the above list, possibly because it is made up of a large number of different disciplines rather than a single, identifiable activity.

A question of origins

You will in the table above that the regions of the world covered by different sports vary considerably. We have already seen that baseball is not followed widely outside the USA, and American football (called NLF – the National Football League – or sometimes Gridiron) even less so. Cricket, while ranking second in the table with a 2.3 billion fan base, is almost unknown in many parts of the world. This is because it originated in England and became widespread in what were Britain's former colonies, such as India, Pakistan and Australia, and some other parts of Asia with colonial connections, such as Bangladesh and Sri Lanka.

Because of the large populations of some of these countries, cricket now enjoys an enormous and passionate fan base. Whether it could be called a truly global sport is a matter for debate, however.

Changes in China

In recent years, China has become more accessible to the West as it seeks to play a more dominant role in global affairs. One outcome of this has been an increased interest in Western sports by the Chinese people. Sports such as football and basketball are now played and followed by millions of Chinese. The Beijing Olympics in 2008 were also hugely influential in opening up athletics and other sports, including basketball, to an enormous Chinese audience. In 2008, a market research poll found that nearly 12 per cent of the urban Chinese are now playing basketball, which is twice the number playing football. At the same time, there has been increased interest in the West in some Eastern sports, such as Chinese martial arts and Sumo wrestling.

Students play basketball in the remote village of Gulucan, Sichuan Province, China. Sports that used to be popular only in the West are now played and followed worldwide. Basketball is the fastest-growing sport in China.

Good or bad?

Some people believe that the globalisation of sport is a good thing; that the sharing of sporting cultures and interests enriches our lives and should be celebrated. Others believe that the globalisation of the sports industry poses a threat to traditional national or local sports. In particular, they believe that Western sporting culture, such as that in the USA and Western Europe, has come to dominate other sporting traditions. They also believe that the need to win and be successful undermines the ideals of sport, such as fair play and genuine competition; in other words, that the globalisation of sport now threatens its very existence.

A growing influence

Sport does not exist in isolation. If there were not people to watch it, sport would remain an important activity, but one that involved relatively few people. Even in ancient Greek and Roman times, sport was a spectator event, drawing and exciting large audiences. In the 7th century BCE, crowds flocked to see the undefeated wrestler, Milo of Croton, compete. Now, a single event, such as the Olympics or the football World Cup, reaches a much wider audience. It has become a global spectacle.

The reason that sport can reach so many people is, of course, television. Television literally brings sport into everyone's living room. With the development of satellite television, such as Fox Sport and Sky Sports, it is now possible to watch sport live almost anywhere in the world. Global television figures are difficult to estimate because of the multitude of channels now available worldwide, but audiences of up to a billion for a single event would not be surprising.

Indian cricket fans watch a live broadcast of the ICC Twenty20 World Cup between Pakistan and India, held in Johannesburg in September 2007, on this giant TV screen.

Media power

The effect of television on the sports industry is to bring sport to new audiences and therefore increase its popularity. This, in turn, opens up an enormous potential market, one that the media and communications industry, particulary advertising, has been quick to exploit. Advertising a product during a major sports competition can bring it to the attention of tens or even hundreds of millions of people. Not surprisingly, then, the income generated by the sale of television rights to certain games and competitions is immense. For example, the American network channel NBC negotiated a package worth US$2.2 billion with the IOC for the American rights to cover the 2008 Olympics in Beijing.

Today, the means by which sports coverage is broadcast extends far beyond television itself. It includes digital interactive television, pay-per-view sport and the internet. For example, in 2008, there were 11.7 million 'unique' users following the Wimbledon Championships on the official Wimbledon website, making 46 million visits. All types of media generate income in different ways, either through direct payment, advertising or, increasingly, online gambling.

A new imperialism?

The globalisation of the sports industry has other impacts through the media and communications industry. Many of the big media companies involved in broadcasting sport are European- or American-owned. Some believe that less developed countries (LDCs) have therefore been subjected to what could be described as a new kind of Western imperialism. This means that they come under the influence of Western ideas and values that may be culturally damaging to the countries concerned. It also means that there is relatively little coverage of sport from Asia, Africa or South America in the West.

Followers of fashion

Like the media and communications industry, the manufacturers of clothes and other sporting goods have been quick to exploit the global influence and attraction of sport. Sportswear is no longer confined to the sports field or gym, but is now considered leisure or fashion wear in its own right.

Clubs gain important revenue through so-called licensing or franchising agreements. This means that they are paid by the company or manufacturer concerned to have their name associated with a particular brand or range of products. In return, global companies, such as Nike or Adidas, get what is known as brand recognition by being associated with the success and prestige of a particular club and its players.

 I'm tired of hearing about money, money, money, money. I just want to play the game, drink Pepsi, wear Reebok.

Shaquille O'Neal, American basketball player, 2002

Sportswear used to be functional – now it is an important part of the global fashion industry. These outfits by Stella McCartney, modelled during London Fashion Week in September 2008, are designed both to look good and to be practical.

Similar arrangements exist for individual sports such as golf, motor racing or tennis. Tiger Woods, for example, has recently signed a US$100 million agreement with the sports drink manufacturer Gatorade, for his own range of sports beverages. Sports clubs and celebrities have been associated with everything from perfumes and shaving products to mobile phones and credit cards.

'Show me the money'

When looking at the distribution of sports around the world, certain patterns emerge. One is that the most successful and well-known sporting teams tend to come from the richer or more developed countries (MDCs). For example, Europe and the USA have tended to dominate football (with the exception of South America), basketball, athletics, golf and motor racing, while the Oceanic countries (Australia, New Zealand and the Pacific islands) have been particularly successful in rugby. Perhaps this is hardly surprising. These countries have the wealth and resources to sustain the sports and to invest in the necessary infrastructure, such as buildings, management structures and grass roots development.

From West to East

Now things are beginning to change. The trend in globalisation generally means that more countries are beginning to appreciate the economic importance of sport, and therefore to develop it. They also understand that sport can bring other benefits, such as tourism, hospitality and investment, which are themselves wealth-creating. Others are less concrete but still important, such as prestige or status, and inclusion as part of the international community. The Middle East and Asia in particular are rapidly becoming important global sporting centres. Sport is one of the examples in which there has been a gradual global shift of power from West to East, from the developed to the less developed world.

SPOTLIGHT

The power of the petrodollar

Petrodollars — money from oil — mainly from the Middle East, but also from Russia, are influencing both the location of sport and the way it is run. In 2007, Dubai announced the fourth major golf tournament to be held in the Gulf States, as part of the so-called European Tour. Total prize money amounted to a staggering US$20 million. Changes like these mean the emphasis of traditionally Western sports has moved away from Europe to follow the money available elsewhere in the world. This is not just about oil wealth, however. As global oil reserves drop, countries such as Dubai, Saudi Arabia, Oman and Kuwait recognise that they need to improve the image of their states, encourage tourism and reduce their dependency on oil and natural gas. They see sport as a way of achieving this.

People on the move

The impact of the globalisation of sport on people can be profound, with both social and cultural consequences. For example, the building of major sports complexes in the Gulf States brings in huge armies of migrant workers from India, Pakistan and Sri Lanka. Many work long shifts on low wages and live in poor working conditions.

Tiger Woods holds the trophy after winning the Dubai 'Desert Classic' Golf Tournament in 2006. Dubai is now one of four Middle Eastern locations that make up part of the so-called 'European' Golf Tour.

In addition, some Gulf States, such as Qatar, have set up soccer scholarship programmes to recruit and train young African footballers in order to groom them for their own national teams. The scale of these operations can be enormous. The Qatar scheme has 6,000 staff assessing more than half a million boys, aged 14, for possible recruitment. Only a few will find success and wealth.

'Passports of convenience'

Other oil-rich countries have used their wealth to tempt African athletes, principally runners, to switch nationality and represent their new host country in competitions (offering them what are known as 'passports of convenience'). Perhaps ironically, the general populations of these countries may show little interest in the sports concerned; rather they are aimed at tourists and wealthy foreigners.

A sustainable industry?

There are many direct environmental impacts of the globalised sports industry, from the building of new infrastructure, such as stadiums, hotels and airports, to the events themselves (see page 35). For big, 'one-off' competitions, such as the Olympic Games, there is also the issue of how well the facilities are used between and after the events – their so-called 'legacy'. After the Sydney Olympics in 2000, plans were drawn up to develop the Sydney Olympic Park for commercial and residential use. Much still remains to be completed on this process, but it is proposed that the site will eventually house 16,500 residents, as well as hotels and banking centres. By contrast, nearly all the venues built for the Athens Olympics in 2004 have fallen into disuse and disrepair.

SPOTLIGHT

London 2012: the most sustainable Games ever?

The authority responsible for the delivery of the London Olympics in 2012 has claimed it will be the most environmentally sustainable Games ever. The Games' sustainability strategy includes:

- **Climate change:** greatly reduced carbon emissions through on-site energy generation and renewable energy;
- **Waste and materials:** 90 per cent of demolition material to be reused or recycled;
- **Transport:** priority given to walking, cycling and the use of public transport to and within the Olympic Park;
- **Biodiversity:** protection and extension of wildlife habitats, especially wetlands, and the creation of the largest new urban park in Europe for 150 years;
- **Regeneration:** community use of facilities and regeneration of local areas after the event; creation of new housing and businesses.

This computer-generated image shows the main Olympic stadium that is under construction for the 2012 London Games. The Games has been promoted as the most sustainable to date.

> *While environmentalism is based on the three Rs – reduce, reuse, recycle – the Games are based on the Big More: more spectators, more sales, more jobs, more tourists, more growth, more infrastructure. This brings enormous contradictions.*
>
> The Guardian, 2 July 2008

A fair return?

Until recently, most goods like sports shoes were produced cheaply, particularly in the Far East, in countries such as Cambodia and Pakistan, where labour conditions were poor and wages low. Child or even slave labour was sometimes involved. Although such abuses still continue, big manufacturers now realise that the negative publicity associated with these practices is bad for business, as well as being morally wrong. Companies like Nike now say they are taking action to ensure such practices do not occur. Nike is also becoming more proactive in reducing the effects of its manufacturing processes on the environment. For example, it runs a recycling programme in which old running shoes are reprocessed into material for running tracks and playgrounds.

These young people in Pakistan are sewing footballs for the Western market. Labourers often work in poor conditions, for little money and receive little or no education. Some of the big sports goods manufacturers are now working to improve such situations.

The future of sport

The sports industry is a medium for bringing people and communities together, both locally and globally. It is also a system of values that is recognised globally and which includes competitive spirit, fair play, the seeking of health and fitness, technical skill and even beauty.

But sport can also be divisive and damaging. People, particularly young men, often develop strong identities with a particular local or national team. This leads to rivalries between groups of supporters, which in turn can lead to violence. Football, in particular, has frequently suffered from violence between fans. Often such confrontations are planned, sometimes over the internet. In the UK, at least, violence between football fans has been much reduced in recent years, largely due to better policing, better 'intelligence' (information about where and when trouble is likely to occur), and better management and separation of supporters in and outside the grounds.

In some other countries, however, football violence is still a major problem. In Argentina, for example, violent behaviour by fans is still common, leading to dangerous stampedes and fights between rival supporters. The country's football authorities are now looking at employing a system, based on biometrics (identification of individuals using physical

SPOTLIGHT

When sport goes bad

In May 2000, the South African cricket captain Hansie Cronje was found guilty of taking bribes from bookmakers in return for giving them 'inside' information about matches they were about to play. He was banned from international cricket as a result. The American sprinter, Marion Jones, admitted in 2007 that she had taken the banned substance THG (an anabolic steroid) during the 2000 Olympic Games in Sydney, where she won three gold and two bronze medals. Her medals were later confiscated. The British runner, Dwayne Chambers, was barred from running in the 2008 Olympics by the British Olympic Committee, despite having already served a two-year ban for taking THG in 2004. Many people believe that athletes found taking drugs should receive a four-year or even life ban. They believe that international bodies such as the IOC and the IAAF (International Association of Athletics Federations) are too weak in exposing drug-taking since they are afraid the adverse publicity will damage the reputation of the sport, and therefore audience figures.

characteristics such as face recognition and fingerprints), to single out potential trouble makers and prohibit them from attending matches.

In it to win it

As sport becomes increasingly global and the money associated with it rises, the pressure to win can become overwhelming. This may involve the taking of illegal, performance-enhancing drugs, and so-called 'match-fixing'. Aspects such as these clearly damage the reputation of the sport concerned, and the sports industry in general.

Sporting success at national level can be a source of pride and inspiration. After the success of Great Britain in the 2008 Olympics, there was renewed interest among young people in the UK, in sports such as swimming and cycling. Greater coverage of events for disabled athletes, such as the Paralympics, has also demonstrated the role of sport in empowering those with physical disabilities to excel and to receive public recognition of their success. As we saw on page 9, sport can be also provide opportunities to those who might otherwise be involved in crime or suffer from low self-esteem.

Good and bad

Sport can be many things. At its best, the sports industry can and should transcend cultural differences and celebrate diversity. At its worst, it creates divisions by reinforcing rivalries between groups and over-emphasising the need to win at all costs. The globalisation of sport makes both of these possibilities more likely.

In the 2000 Olympic Games in Sydney, Australia, Cathy Freeman became the first Aboriginal athlete to both represent her country and win a gold medal, winning the women's 400 metres.

Manchester United: a global brand

Manchester United Football Club is the highest-valued sports club in the world, at around US$1.8 billion. It is also one of the best known. Its fans come from almost everywhere in the world, although only a tiny minority have ever seen the club actually play. Manchester United has some of the best-known and highest-paid players, both past and present. You may have heard of legendary players such as Bobby Charlton and George Best. More recently, great players such as Eric Cantona (France), David Beckham (England) and the Portuguese player Cristiano Ronaldo have excited supporters worldwide. Players such as these have been able to transcend the game of football itself, and become international celebrities in their own right.

In the 1960s, the Manchester United footballer George Best (centre) became internationally famous, not only for his superb football skills, but also for his association with different fashion products and his lavish lifestyle off the pitch.

Team history

What is it that has made Manchester United itself one of the most recognised and successful clubs in the world? How has it become what we would now call a global brand? The answer harks back to a dark and freezing night in Germany in 1958. Returning from a successful European Cup match (now the UEFA Champion's League) against Red Star Belgrade, the plane carrying the Manchester United team crashed on take-off from Munich airport. Eight of the players died in the crash.

Despite the terrible loss of its team members, the club battled on to reach the final of the FA Cup in the same year. A decade later, Manchester United became the first English club to win the European Cup. That accident, all those years ago, marked the start of a legend that has been growing ever since. But a legend does not happen automatically. The rise of Manchester United as a global force in football has been carefully managed and nurtured both on and off the football field.

Competition	Winning years
FA Premier League	1965, 1967,1993, 1994, 1996, 1997, 1999, 2000, 2001, 2003, 2007, 2008
FA Challenge Cup ('FA Cup')	1963, 1977, 1983, 1985,1990, 1994,1996, 1999, 2004
Football League Cup	1992, 2006
European Cup	1968, 1999, 2008
(UEFA Champions' League) European Cup Winners Cup	1991
(UEFA Cup) European Super Cup	1991
International Cup	1999
FA Community Shield (League winner against (FA cup winner)	1965, 1967, 1977, 1983,1990, 1993, 1994, 1996, 1997, 2003, 2007

Competitions won by Manchester United between 1958 and 2008 are listed here. Since the formation of the English Premier League in 1992, there have been only four years in which the club has failed to win either a domestic (UK) or European title.

A new beginning?

In 1992 the English Premier League (EPL) was formed. This was a group of England's top 20 football clubs which, as well as Manchester United, included other great clubs such as Liverpool and Tottenham Hotspur. The aim was to create a new 'super league' that would attract not only larger audiences, but greater income. Similar developments were occurring in other parts of Europe, such as Germany and Italy, where the top league in each case could command increasingly huge television and sponsorship deals. Football was about to become a global commodity.

A visitor inspects Manchester United's impressive trophy cabinet. Part of the club's recognition as a global brand has been due to its consistent performance over many years.

PERSPECTIVES FOR DEBATE

"Over recent years, we have seen unfair terms and huge ticket price rises imposed on supporters by club owners taking advantage of their loyalty."

Duncan Drasdo, Chief Executive of Manchester United Supporters' Trust, 2008

"I thought that was unfair and inaccurate because as we all know the prices at Arsenal and Chelsea are absolutely obscene... They are almost double our prices."

Sir Alex Ferguson, Manager of Manchester United, replying to a government minister's accusation that high ticket prices were 'obscene' and pricing ordinary fans out of the game, 2008

Trouble ahead?

The road to success for the new EPL was far from simple. In 1995, the European Court of Justice passed a law that meant that British clubs no longer had to observe the so-called 'maximum of three foreign players rule'. This, together with other changes, meant that European-born players could now move freely to any club within Europe, as their contracts expired. The result was fierce competition among the clubs for top-class players. More recently, this freedom of movement was extended to other countries such as those in Africa and South America (although such movement has now become more restricted, due to the introduction of a points system based on international playing experience). The players themselves could negotiate huge salaries and transfer deals. In order to pay for this, clubs like Manchester United realised they would have to increase the 'marketability' of their teams. This meant widening their appeal to spectators, sponsors, sports goods manufacturers (merchandising) and television viewers – and they needed to do this on a global scale.

Appealing to spectators

For years, many football stadiums were unwelcoming and poorly maintained venues, where most of the supporters were crammed, standing, onto so-called terraces. The crowds were often unprotected from the elements and the facilities were poor. Following a tragedy at an FA Cup semi-final match at the Hillsborough stadium in Sheffield in 1989, where 95 spectators were crushed to death, stadiums were required to be all-seater venues. As a result, clubs were forced to generally improve their facilities, making them more attractive to supporters.

Manchester United was no exception. The Old Trafford stadium in the centre of the city is now the largest club venue in the UK, with a capacity of nearly 76,000 people. Included in this are special facilities for 2,400 corporate customers, bringing in valuable business revenue to the club. The club also has its own television studios and provides facilities for regular supporters in order to make the experience of visiting the ground more memorable for them – and more profitable for the club. This includes restaurants, a museum, a megastore selling club merchandise, and illuminated advertising displays around the pitch.

Not everyone has been happy with these developments, however. In 2005, the club was taken over by an American businessman, Malcolm Glazer. Fans complained that ticket prices had risen sharply, despite the club's economic success. This led to protests outside the club and calls for a boycott of club merchandise. In 2008, Man U fans called for an investigation into ticket price increases, claiming that some prices had risen by as much as 60 per cent. Many thought the club was being developed as part of a global business empire, rather than as a famous sporting institution.

Attracting sponsors

A key to Manchester United's success has been its ability to draw in sponsors. A successful club is attractive to manufacturers and businesses that want to be associated with the club's achievements. In May 2006, United signed a four-year, £56 million deal with the American insurance giant AIG (American Insurance Group). A big club needs more than one sponsor, however. In 2002, United had signed a 13-year deal worth a staggering £303 million with the sportswear manufacturer Nike. The list of sponsors is likely to grow as big clubs like Manchester United seek deals with companies in individual countries.

Sponsor	Nationality and interest
AIG	American Insurance corporation
Nike	American sports wear manufacturer
Betfred	UK bookmaker
Hublot	Swiss watch company
Kumho	South Korean tyre company
Budweiser	American beer manufacturer
STC	Saudi Arabian telecommunications company
Hi Seoul	South Korean travel company
Viagogo	London-based European ticket company

These were the official sponsors of Manchester United in 2008. The total worth of sponsorship runs to nearly £40 million a year. You can judge the global nature of Man U's business by the range of countries represented.

Manchester United's Portuguese player Cristiano Ronaldo celebrates scoring a goal. Some of United's sponsors can be seen on the display panels around the pitch and on the players' kit.

Merchandising, merchandising

The idea of selling goods bearing the name of successful sports clubs became widespread in the early 1990s. The extent and reach of what is known as merchandising expanded to global proportions. At that time, Man U formed the trading company Manchester United Merchandising Limited. The company sells sports goods and other products through its megastore at its Old Trafford ground and, more importantly, through its own website which links to thousands of associated websites around the world. Annual turnover of these products worldwide is now in the region of £20 million.

A Manchester United fan's bedroom. The worldwide merchandising of club-related products, such as jerseys, scarves, and even bed-covers, has become an important generator of income for big clubs like United.

These developments have been criticised by people who claim fans feel pressured into buying products, such as new ranges of kit. Some fans in particular feel that, under the club's new ownership, the emphasis on merchandising has gone too far. They want to see a return to what they view as the true purpose of the club: winning trophies and supporting football at the local level. Others believe that, without these additional revenues, the club would not be able to continue to operate in a global environment.

Competing for viewers

Television is a global medium. In the late 1980s, the media tycoon Rupert Murdoch offered a staggering £304 million to top football clubs to broadcast their matches live on his Sky Sports satellite channel. This was followed by a further four-year contract until 1997, worth £670 million. Current contracts are worth over £1 billion.

Manchester United was quick to see the benefits of having its matches broadcast to a global audience. It also added to its outreach by creating its own television network, MUTV, in 1999. Through this medium it could also promote its own club products and services.

Through further media deals with Rupert Murdoch's Fox Sport and Direct TV channels, EPL clubs such as Manchester United also gained access to a growing interest in soccer in North America: and with a further agreement with an Asian media group, they entered another 150 million households in Asia. Today, it is estimated that the EPL reaches an audience of 1 billion viewers (almost a sixth of the world's population) in over 170 countries. Manchester United is at the forefront of this global exposure.

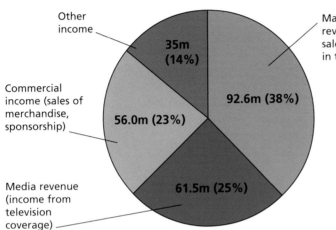

Other income — 35m (14%)

Match day revenue (ticket sales and sales in the ground

Commercial income (sales of merchandise, sponsorship) — 56.0m (23%)

92.6m (38%)

Media revenue (income from television coverage) — 61.5m (25%)

Manchester United's annual income for 2007 amounted to a total of £245 million. Perhaps surprisingly, most revenue still comes from ticket and other sales on match days.

SPOTLIGHT

The Asian connection

Manchester United estimates it has about 40 million fans in Asia (over half the global total of Man U fans). Much of this has resulted from the increased popularity of the sport within the region, due to a range of factors, such as visiting English teams, China qualifying for the 2002 World Cup (hosted in South Korea and Japan), and the signing of a number of Asian players by clubs in the EPL. United has built on these interests by playing exhibition games in Asia, signing sponsorship deals with Asian companies, establishing Asian outlets for club merchandise, and supporting Asian soccer schools and academies.

Manchester United – a global brand

Manchester United's success has been the result of careful planning and an understanding of how 'the global market' works. Equally important, however, has been the ability of the club to portray itself as a powerful symbol that goes far beyond football – what we would now call its iconic status. What perhaps started in a tragedy in a snow-covered airport over 50 years ago has since gone on to become an example of a truly global industry.

Athletics at the Beijing Olympics

Although athletics itself does not appear in the top ten list of sports (see page 10), there can be little doubt that its central position in the Olympic Games makes it a global sport. The Beijing Olympics in 2008 saw some of the most dramatic races in Olympic history, including the breaking of three world records by a single athlete, the Jamaican sprinter, Usain Bolt.

A global event

Many people felt that the organisation of the 2008 Olympic Games itself was a success – it was certainly the most expensive and spectacular. The opening and closing ceremonies set new standards for sheer brilliance and theatre. A total of 37 venues, 12 of them newly constructed, were used for events. Most dramatic of these was the Beijing National Stadium, nicknamed the 'Birds Nest', where the majority of the events were held. In all, an estimated US$42 billion was spent on the games, making it by far the most expensive games ever. The global TV audience was estimated at 4.7 billion over the duration of the Games. In China itself, 94 per cent of all viewers were tuned to the Olympics.

Part of the opening ceremony at the Beijing Olympics in August 2008. The ceremony was praised for its drama and spectacle, but also criticised for being too lavish and expensive.

Big numbers

A total of 10,500 athletes competed in 302 events in 28 different sports at the Beijing Olympics. The Games saw 43 new world records and 132 Olympic records. Chinese athletes won 51 gold medals, more than any other country. Two new Olympic teams, the Marshall Islands and Tuvalu, competed in the Games, and Serbia and Montenegro competed separately for the first time, following the splitting of these two former Yugoslavian countries in 2006. An estimated 450,000–500,000 overseas visitors were expected to attend the Games. In the event, however, the high price of travel and accommodation, and heavy security restrictions, meant that this number was probably not achieved.

New infrastructure

The Olympic venues and ceremonies were not the only expense. In order for the Games to run smoothly, a vast amount of infrastructure had to be built or improved. Almost all of Beijing's transportation systems underwent expansion, including a major development of Beijing's airport. This comprised the construction of a new terminal, a new railway station, and the upgrading of the 120 kilometres Beijing-Tianjin Intercity Rail, connecting the new station with the Olympic co-host city, Tianjin. In addition, Beijing's subway system (underground railway) was more than doubled in size. Fleets of thousands of buses were put into service to transport spectators, athletes and officials between venues.

Clearing the air

The Games had another side, however. Beijing is notorious for its air pollution, resulting from the enormous flow of city traffic and its industrial emissions. Many athletes, particularly those in long distance events, were concerned for their health. Before and during the Games, a 'traffic rationing' system was put in place, based on car number plates, and heavily polluting vehicles were banned from the city. It was hoped that the improved public transport systems would absorb the demands of both visitors and commuters alike. In the event, the combination of these measures, and favourable weather conditions, meant that the air quality was reasonable throughout the Games.

Trouble at the Games

Air pollution was not the only issue to trouble the Games. The choice of China as the host country itself was a controversial one. Despite China's increased openness to the West, and the greater freedom it allowed its people, many felt that its record on human rights – that is, how it treated its own people and those under its control – did not justify awarding it the Games. They felt this gave recognition to a regime that was still unacceptable in its behaviour. In particular, they objected to the way in which China treated its neighbour, Tibet. China maintains that Tibet is part of China, while many both inside and outside the country disagree. Before and during the Games there were a number of demonstrations against China, some of which were dealt with brutally by the Chinese authorities.

Demonstrators in San Francisco shout protests against China's treatment of Tibet before the arrival of the Olympic torch.

Another criticism was the fact that, despite China's rapid development, many of its people still live in poverty and deprivation. Many people questioned the huge amounts of money being spent on the Games rather than on improving living conditions for many of China's own people. In addition, a severe earthquake in May of the same year meant that many thousands of victims of the disaster were still homeless at the time of the event.

Relatives mourn the death of a victim of the Dujiangyan earthquake in China in May 2008. The earthquake killed over 1000 people and made hundreds of thousands homeless. The Chinese authorities were heavily criticised for not giving more help to the region when billions of dollars were being spent on the Olympic Games.

Others felt that it was important to 'embrace' China; that awarding them the Games would encourage the country to continue to bring about reforms and draw it further into the international community. Against this, however, were those who felt that commercial considerations were now overshadowing moral choices. Whatever else the Games achieved, they showed that it was impossible to separate global sport from global politics.

A new beginning?

Many people took the view that, once the Games had been awarded to Beijing, they had to go ahead, whatever the political and moral implications. It was also agreed, however, that lessons needed to be learned. One was that we should not be surprised when a host country 'uses' the Games to promote itself and its policies on such a large global stage. Another was that the competition to make each Games more spectacular than the last was putting enormous pressure on the host country's resources. It is likely that future Games, including London in 2012, will scale down some of the events and ceremonies, as well as making them more sustainable (see page 16). This may signal a return to the Olympic ideal that makes athletics and the Olympic Games not just a global industry, but a global activity in which all can take part.

PERSPECTIVES FOR DEBATE

"The winning of the 2008 Olympic bid is an example of the international recognition of China's social stability, economic progress and the healthy life of the Chinese people"

Li Lanqing, Vice-premier, People's Republic of China, 2005

"The governments of democratic countries that are still hoping the Olympic Games will help to improve the human right situation in China are mistaken. The 'constructive dialogue' advocated by some is leading nowhere."

Reporters without Frontiers website, 2008

Formula One: an industry on the move

CASE STUDY UNCOVERED

It is easy to understand why Formula One (F1) racing attracts huge numbers of followers, both at the tracks themselves and through the broadcasting of live events. Formula One combines great drama and spectacle with enormous technical skill, both behind the wheel and in the workshops and test tracks where the cars are developed. When the young British driver Lewis Hamilton (driving a McLaren Mercedes) won the 2008 World Championship by a single point over the Brazilian Felipe Massa of the Ferrari team at the Brazilian Grand Prix, the scenes of celebration and despair, by teams and spectators alike, were equally emotional.

The young British driver Lewis Hamilton won the 2008 F1 World Championship by a single point. The excitement and drama of F1 racing has made it a huge spectacle around the world.

Formula for success?

Today, Formula One is one of the most competitive, highly technical and high-cost industries in the world. A top team such as McLaren or BMW will spend more than US$500 million in a season and employ more than 500 people, ranging from marketing and commercial experts to engineers and scientists, as well as the race team itself.

In the UK alone, more than 4,000 hi-tech engineering businesses depend on motorsport in some way. The industry as a whole has an estimated turnover of US$4 billion, employs 50,000 people in more than 30 countries and is followed in every major economy of the world. It is estimated that over 6 billion people watch Grand Prix (GP) events over the course of a year (18 or 19 races). Much of this has been due to a rapidly expanding global television audience.

The rise of Formula One

In order to understand how Formula One has developed into a global industry, and to gain some insights into its future, we need to look at its origins. The first F1 race was held at the Silverstone race track in England in the UK in 1950. At that time there were only six races in the season, all in Europe with the exception of Indianapolis, in the USA. The Italian car-maker Alfa Romeo dominated the championship, but it would soon be replaced by Ferrari and then Mercedes Benz, driven by the legendary Argentine driver, Juan Manuel Fangio.

Driving funds

Technology has dominated the development of F1 as much as great racing drivers, however. The high cost of developing and running a successful team has meant that smaller, independent racing teams, such as Lotus and Stewart, have gradually been replaced by the big manufacturers such as Mercedes, Ferrari, BMW and Renault. One way to fund the cost of racing, of course, is sponsorship. In 1968, the Lotus 49 became the first F1 car to appear in a sponsor's 'livery' (its colours and brand name) – in this case, a tobacco company. Since that time, F1 has had a close relationship with the tobacco industry, although this has recently declined, with stricter controls on advertising.

Sharing the excitement

The drama and danger of Grand Prix racing has been exploited by television companies. In the early 1990s, lightweight TV cameras were attached to the cars themselves to give viewers a real taste of what it was like to drive at over 200 miles per hour! Soon after that, the widespread use of satellite television meant that F1 was on its way to becoming not just a thrilling spectacle, but a global industry.

The spread of F1 competitions in schools has also added to the global phenomenon that F1 has become. For example, the competition F1 in Schools started in the UK in 1999, challenging students aged 9–19 to design, construct, test and race a to-scale, gas-powered Formula One car. In 2009, the UK national champions won a tour of the Williams F1 team headquarters and one member of the team is guaranteed a chance to work within the Williams Formula One Team. The winning team also goes on to the Schools World Championship to compete with 30 other countries worldwide.

Going global

Something else in F1 was changing. In 1973, the Interlagos track in Brazil was added to the list of Grand Prix venues, meaning that the sport was no longer restricted to Europe and North America. This was followed by Japan in 1976. In 1985, Australia hosted F1 for the first time (at that time in Adelaide, but it is now held in Melbourne). Other new venues quickly followed, in Hungary (1986) as the so-called Iron Curtain countries became more liberated, and then, some years later, in Turkey (2005). Meanwhile, the Middle and Far East were also becoming important Grand Prix fixtures. In 2004, a new race in Bahrain made its debut and this was followed in the same year by a race in China. In 2008, Singapore staged a night-time Formula One event, the first ever to be held under floodlights. A night start in Singapore meant that the race could be seen live on television in the West at a more reasonable time.

The 2008 Grand Prix in Singapore was the first to be run at night.

These new venues partly reflect the rapid emergence of Eastern countries as they become an increasingly important part of the world economy. At the same time, some of the more traditional GP venues have been losing their grip on the sport. The famous Indianapolis race track in the USA was lost from the F1 calender in 2008, while the popular Gilles Villeneuve track in Canada disappeared from the schedule in the following year. The reasons for these changes were not clear. The most likely reason was that the organisers of F1 and the managers of the tracks were unable to come to an agreement over terms (see page 34). Whatever the case, it meant that North America no longer hosted a Formula One event for the first time in over 40 years.

It's all about the money

As with all major sports, sponsorship, branding and merchandising on a global scale have been vital to the growth of the F1 industry. International companies are willing to pay vast sums to have their brands on Formula One cars. Teams such as McLaren and Williams get 80–85 per cent of their total income from sponsorship; the rest comes from TV revenue and prize money.

SPOTLIGHT

You get what you pay for

Title sponsors (US$15–50million): a company has its brand included in the official title of the team, for example, Red Bull-Renault or Toro Rosso-Ferrari; their name is positioned on all the highest-profile parts of the car that get most television exposure.

Co-sponsor (US$3–15million): these are backers who want the prestige of being linked with a sport with a high-tech, modern image. They are usually media, finance or engineering companies, such as the finance company Santander and car manufacturer McLaren. They get good, but less prominent, coverage on the car.

Trade link-ups (US$1–3million): these are companies, such as suppliers, who are more interested in being able to associate themselves with the image of the team. They may have small spaces in parts of the car like the side of the rear wing, or the wing mirrors.

Mechanics surround the Formula One racecar of driver Felipe Massa in the Ferrari pits at the Australian Grand Prix in 2008.

Under pressure

F1 has an exciting and colourful image. Racing drivers are treated like celebrities around the world and both they and their teams attract a huge and passionate following. The industry is not without its problems, however. In the early 2000s, Ferrari's dominance of the sport led to some 'staged' finishes, in which the team's two drivers were instructed to finish in a particular order, to maintain their position at the top of both the drivers' and constructors' championship. TV ratings and attendance at events noticeably declined as this 'win at all costs' attitude seemed to take over from real competition.

In 2005, the EU banned the advertising of tobacco on cars and this threatened the future of the sport in Europe, since other regions of the world were less concerned about tobacco sponsorship. Some people believe the expansion of the sport beyond Europe was at least partly due to the need to maintain this source of revenue for as long as possible.

These men, Bernie Ecclestone on the left and Max Moseley on the right, are the two most powerful players in Formula One and, between them, control both how and where F1 is run.

Management issues

In addition, there has been much criticism of the management of Formula One and its domination by a small number of key people within it. Max Moseley is the president of the Fédération Internationale de l'Automobile (FIA), which governs the way F1 and other types of motor racing are controlled and run. Bernie Ecclestone is the president of the Formula One Group of companies. As such, he can negotiate the F1 Grand Prix programme, particularly the race venues, and how much a particular location is charged.

It has been suggested that they wield too much power, for example in deciding new race venues, and that this will ultimately damage the sport. However, both men are expected to retire in the next few years. These examples highlight that there is a question mark over the ability of F1 to continue to develop as a sport that is seen to be both fair and above purely commercial interests (see page 33).

A greener future?

F1 also has to address issues of sustainability. Like any major sport, motor racing attracts large crowds and demands major infrastructure. The night-run Grand Prix in Singapore attracted criticism for its enormous use of energy in lighting the event. The cars themselves consume large amounts of fuel and, until recently, a single team could get through over 900 tyres in a season (at £1,500 a time!).

Many people in the sport itself believe that F1 can become a high-tech pioneer in addressing climate change and waste. Proposals include smaller engines, using biofuel, paddocks run by solar power and restricting the use of energy-consuming wind tunnels during testing. By 2011, F1 will introduce a number of major changes to conserve fuel. These include employing a mechanism that mimics how modern electric hybrid cars work. Engine revolutions ('revs') will also be limited and there will be a ban on engine testing except for during practice on a race weekend.

Uncertainty ahead

Critics think that the whole point of motor racing will be compromised by sustainable choices; that faster speeds and winning races must remain the ultimate goal. The future of F1 is therefore at a crossroads. In February 2007, Honda announced it was stopping sponsorship identification on its cars. Instead, its new RA107 model was covered in artwork depicting the planet Earth and a website promoting its new environmental charity, 'My Earth Dreams'. However, in December 2008, Honda announced it was quitting F1 because of the 'downturn' in the global economy, and because of its relatively poor performance. Only time will tell if F1 can continue to develop as a sustainable, affordable and genuine competition – and maintain its hold on its global audience.

Interest in motor racing, and F1 in particular, has stimulated the growth of karting among young people.

Tennis: a global power for good?

The international body that governs tennis, the International Tennis Federation (ITF), claims that tennis is 'one of the few truly global sports'. Few would argue with this. When Rafael Nadal of Spain beat Roger Federer of Switzerland in the Wimbledon final in July 2008, the match was watched live by 13.1 million viewers in the UK alone and an estimated 200 million worldwide. Meanwhile, the women's final was contested by two Americans, the Williams sisters. Despite the American and European presence in the finals, however, other countries are now beginning to dominate the game. The tide in tennis is moving east, to Eastern Europe, Russia, and beyond.

Raphael Nadal of Spain plays a stroke on his way to beating the Swiss player Roger Federer in the Wimbledon 2008 men's finals.

A sport for all?

The ITF makes the following statement about its role in promoting tennis:

> The objective of the ITF is to further grow and develop the sport worldwide, to develop the game at all levels at all ages for both able-bodied and disabled men and women... to preserve the integrity and independence of tennis as a sport, and to perform all this without discrimination...
>
> ITF website

Almost every country in the world has a national tennis association linked to the ITF. They are divided into six regions: Asia, South America, Central America and the Caribbean, Africa, Oceania and Europe (the USA and Canada are members of the ITF but not included in the six regions). The ITF controls the major international team events for all age groups and for wheelchair tennis. These include the two main events, the Davis Cup for men and the Fed (originally Federation) Cup for women. The ITF also controls the four major annual tennis tournaments, the so-called Grand Slams: Wimbledon, and the US, French and Australian Opens.

Power to the players?

Many people would argue that the real power in tennis lies not with the ITF, but with the players themselves. Like other sports stars who have achieved global status, players like Roger Federer, Maria Sharapova and the Williams sisters enjoy worldwide recognition and celebrity. They are known and recognised far beyond the immediate world of tennis, and are in constant demand by sponsors and manufacturers to endorse their products. In January 2008, Maria Sharapova signed a multi-million, four-year sponsorship deal with the telecommunications giant Sony Ericsson to become 'the company's first global brand ambassador'. Later in that year, the Spanish player Rafael Nadal launched his own fragrance line after signing a deal with the fashion and perfume company, Lanvin.

Former Wimbledon Champion, Maria Sharapova, poses on the red carpet at a Sony Ericsson players' party in Florida. Global companies, like Sony, are now central to the development of tennis as a global industry.

SPOTLIGHT

Top-earning tennis players (2008)

• **Roger Federer** (Switzerland): US$35 million; including US$9 million in prize money, the rest in sponsorship; sponsors include Gillette, Mercedes-Benz and Wilson (tennis rackets); his agreement with Nike is for ten years and will probably be the largest in tennis history.

• **Maria Sharapova** (Russia): US$26 million; most of her earnings came from sponsorship and endorsements in 2008; sponsors include Canon, Colgate-Palmolive (pharmaceuticals), Sony Ericsson, Tag Heuer (watches) and Tiffany (Jewellery).

• **Rafael Nadal** (Spain): US$18 million; took over from Roger Federer as world number one in 2008; sponsors include Nike and the South Korean car manufacturer, Kia.

• **Andy Roddick** (USA): US$15 million; the highest-ranked American player since Pete Sampras and Andre Agassi; sponsors include Lacoste (clothes and shoes), Lexus (part of Toyota) and SAP (business software).

• **Venus and Serena Williams** (USA): US$15 million each; Serena Williams is sponsored by Nike, while her sister has her own tennis and casual clothing line. Serena Williams' agreement with Nike is worth US$55 million over five years.

Players' associations

Much of the players' power comes through their own professional associations. In the case of men, this is the Association of Tennis Professionals (ATP) and for women, the Women's Tennis Association (WTA). These bodies organise what are known as the ATP and WTA World Tours, a string of worldwide tennis tournaments involving the top players in the world. These organisations also decide the individual rankings of players and this, in turn, determines their 'value' to sponsors.

Like many other sports bodies, however, the ATP and the WTA also rely heavily on sponsorship. In 2005, the WTA signed a six-year deal with Sony Ericsson, worth US$88 million. Until 2008, the ATP was sponsored by the car giant, Mercedes Benz. The players' associations also negotiate television rights. In 2001, the ATP began buying up advertising slots from the companies that screen its tournaments, such as CBS, ESPN and European broadcasters, in a deal to secure advertising space for its own sponsors.

SPOTLIGHT

Tennis sponsorship – the African connection

2009 saw the first ATP World Tour tournament to be held in Africa. The event, held in South Africa, is part of a US$22 million sponsorship package by South African Airways (SAA), which includes its role as the official airline for the Tour. According to the head of SAA, Khaya Ngqula, the event will be a major boost for the sport in Africa and strengthens the ATP's presence in 'a key global market'.

From Russia (and beyond) with love

For much of its history, professional tennis has been dominated by American, European and Australian players, such as Pete Sampras, Chris Evert, Bjorn Borg and, in the early 1960s when tennis became fully professional, Rod Laver. In recent years, however, the tide has turned towards the East. With the opening up of the former Soviet Union (now Russia and a number of surrounding countries) and Eastern Europe, players such as Jelena Jankovic (Serbia), Elena Dementieva (Russia), Novak Djokovic (Serbia) and Nikolay Davydenko (Russia) have moved into the top rankings. At the end of 2008, seven out of the top ten women players in the world were from Russia and Eastern Europe.

Serbian player Novak Djokovic wins the Shanghai Masters Cup in November 2008, making him the third-ranking player in the world. Players from Eastern Europe now rival their American and western European counterparts.

> Keep going global. It's great to see Asia becoming a big player, and I'm hoping Africa becomes a big player in the next 10 years. It's about giving kids an opportunity so they can get the same feeling we get, of hitting the perfect shot.
>
> Martina Navratilova, nine-times Wimbledon women's singles champion, 2008

The move east has not stopped there, however. Players like Paradom Srichaphan from Thailand have recently featured in the top 50 for the men's game, while Chinese players are beginning to make an impact in women's tennis.

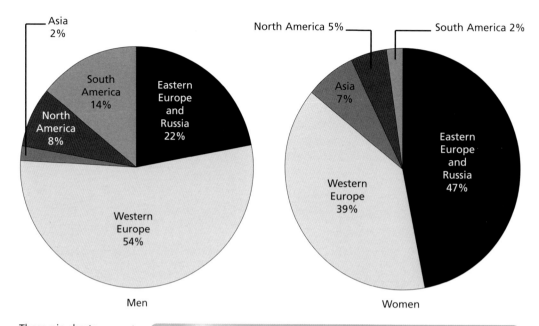

Asia 2%
South America 14%
North America 8%
Eastern Europe and Russia 22%
Western Europe 54%

Men

North America 5%
South America 2%
Asia 7%
Eastern Europe and Russia 47%
Western Europe 39%

Women

These pie charts show the nationality of top 100 men and women tennis players (based on Feb 2009 ratings). Western European men still dominate the men's game but the largest proportion of women players now come from Eastern Europe and Russia. North American players are no longer well represented in either game, while Asian women players are now beginning to have more impact. Australian players are absent from both groups.

SPOTLIGHT

China's tennis aces cash in on success

Chinese tennis players will get to keep more of their winnings to encourage them to raise their game on the international stage. In the past, Chinese athletes have had to hand over most of their earnings to their coaches and their national associations. Now, Chinese players are entitled to 70 per cent of their winnings, while top talents like China's number one Li Na and Wimbledon semi-finalist Zjeng Jie are eligible for more if they do well at Grand Slams and other big tournaments.

Working from the grass roots

A truly global sport is played at all levels and in all communities. This is not just to feed into the professional game or create future national or international stars. It is also about recognising the role sport plays in promoting health and fitness and developing communities. In the USA, for example, the United States Tennis Association (USTA), like all national associations, promotes and develops tennis at all levels. Tennis is one of the few sports in the USA that is currently showing increased participation at community level. In the UK, the Tennis Foundation works within the national governing body, the Lawn Tennis Association (LTA), to perform a similar task. This includes introducing tennis to all ages and abilities, creating a strategy to involve school and park tennis, promoting indoor tennis and supporting disabled teams. In the past 15 years, 300,000 primary school children have benefited from the scheme.

More equal than others?

In 2007, Wimbledon became the last of the Grand Slam competitions to agree to pay equal prize money to both male and female competitors. The subject of equal pay in sport generally has been hotly debated for many years. In terms of tennis, the Wimbledon organisers argued that, since men played more sets than women (up to five per match rather than three), the difference was justified. This argument was dismissed by others as simply ridiculous.

In 2008, UNESCO and the WTA Tour promoters announced that one of the most famous and successful women players of all time, Billie Jean King, had been appointed 'Global Mentor for Gender Equality'. King campaigned for equal pay throughout her career, and has since founded an organisation called the Women's Sports Foundation, with a mission to increase opportunity and participation for women and girls in sport. The pairing of WTA and UNESCO, however, had a wider purpose: to 'further gender equality and promote women's leadership in all spheres of society'. Projects include night school programs for girls in Liberia, the creation of a group of successful female politicians, and a program in the Dominican Republic to train young women in leadership skills. A global sport has finally taken a stand on a global issue.

PERSPECTIVES FOR DEBATE

"We could respond to the pressures and do something that is fundamentally unfair to the men, but we have not."

Tim Phillips, Chairman of the All England Club/Wimbledon, 2006

"They [Wimbledon] are clearly trying to make a statement. On the one hand, they say they cherish the players....and on the other hand, they are telling the world that Venus Williams is less of a champion than Roger Federer."

Larry Scott, chief executive of the Sony Ericsson WTA Tour, 2006

Tennis starts at the grass roots; young players like these in Nairobi, Kenya, may become the stars of the future.

Becoming an active global citizen

What is an active global citizen? It is someone who tries, in their own small way, to make the world a better place. To become an active global citizen, you will need to get involved in decisions that others make about your life and the lives of others around the world. Consider how the world could be changed, such as improving the environment, political or social conditions for others, and seek information about the issues from a wide variety of sources. Then go public by presenting your arguments to others, from classmates and local groups, to national politicians and global organisations.

In your life

This section is not really about becoming more sporting as such; it is more about the things you can do in terms of being an active global citizen in relation to sport and the sporting industry.

• Start an activity yourself.

Is there a lack of sporting or activity-based facilities or opportunities in your area? Get a small group of friends together to see what can be done; you could carry out a local survey of young people to get their views. You might decide to campaign for a particular facility, or you may even be able to start up a new activity yourself. Creating change is never easy and you need a good idea of what you want to achieve and how you might go about it. You may well need adult help – talk to teachers, leisure centre staff or youth leaders to see how they might be involved.

• Take an interest in a sport-related issue.

As we have seen in this book, there are many important issues surrounding sport, especially in a global context. For instance, girls' and women's participation in sport is often not valued as highly as male sport and taken less seriously, particularly by the media. Some cultures expressly forbid women's participation in sport or at least discourage it. Carry out more research in this or another issue.

• Be aware of what is happening.

Take a greater interest in the real stories and issues behind the sporting headlines. Sport is often treated superficially by the media – it often concentrates on sporting celebrities or on high profile teams. As we have seen, modern sport is a highly complex and commercial activity, and it operates at many different levels. This is what makes sport so interesting, but you need to be prepared to dig beneath the surface!

Key terms for internet searches

Type these terms into a search engine on the internet and see what results you get. How many hits appear? Are the websites from around the world, and are there any sources that surprise you?

- Community Sports (then add your local area)
- FIA (Fédération Internationale d'Automobile)
- FIFA (Fédération Internationale de Football Association)
- Global sports
- IOC (International Olympic Committee)
- LTA (Lawn Tennis Association)
- London Olympics
- Media and sport
- Nike/sponsorship
- Sport and disability
- Sustainability and sport
- Women's sport

Data watch

Keep on top of global statistics by visiting these websites below.

• Biggest sporting stadiums	http://www.forbes.com/2008/11/25/stadiums-racing-football-biz-sports_cx_tvr_1125stadiums.html
• English Premier League stats	http://www.premierleague.com
• Formula 1 circuits	http://uk.eurosport.yahoo.com/f1/circuits
• Manchester United stats and news	http://www.manutd.com
• Men's tennis rankings and tournaments	http://www.atptennis.com
• Olympic games stats and news	http://www.olympic.org/uk
• Sporting records	http://www.guinessworldrecords.com
• The world's best paid athletes	http://www.msnbc.msn.com/id/11961246/

Topic web

Use this topic web to discover the themes and ideas in subject areas related to the sports industry.

English
- Discuss in pairs or small groups whether China should have been allowed to stage the 2008 Olympic Games.
- Describe the sensations you might experience during the final lap of a Grand Prix, either as a spectator, a driver, or the head of an F1 team like McLaren).

Citizenship
- Track a particular sporting event in a range of newspapers and see how its coverage varies between papers.
- Examine how sport is viewed by different cultures or religions.
- Debate the pros and cons of 'passports of convenience' (see page 15); do they allow athletes from LDCs to obtain a better life for themselves and their families, or do they exploit the athletes and their country of origin?
- Discuss the benefits of community sports.
- Investigate the economics of a major sporting club, such as Real Madrid or the New York Yankees, including sponsorship, television rights and merchandising. To what extent does the source of funding affect the way the sport is conducted?

Science
- Investigate the environmental issues surrounding the London Olympics (see page 16).
- Research some of the technical detail behind running an F1 team such as McLaren or Ferrari, and the proposals for improving the sustainability of the industry.

Art
- Consider how sport is portrayed in art or photography.

The Sports Industry

Geography
- Research the world distribution of a named global sport and suggest some of the reasons for that distribution.
- Look at how the infrastructure of a particular sport differs in an LDC and an MDC. Does location truly

History
- Write an account of how a major sport like football or tennis has changed over time, from a largely non-professional (amateur) activity to a highly professional global industry.
- Chart the changes in popularity of a particular sport, such as swimming or cycling, as a community-based activity.

PE
- Investigate the training regime and diet of a modern athlete; how have these changed since Roger Bannister ran the first sub-four-minute mile in 1954?

Glossary

anabolic steroids a group of manufactured chemicals, similar to the male hormone, testosterone, used illegally by some athletes to improve performance; they may have damaging side effects.

brand a product name, such as Nike or AIG, which is easily recognised by the public. Brand recognition occurs when a product or manufacturer becomes well-known enough to be instantly recognisable.

European Court of Justice the highest court of the EU, with the ultimate say on matters of EU law to ensure they are equally applied across all member states.

Fédération Internationale de l'Automobile (FIA) the international governing body for world motor sport and motoring organisations.

Fédération Internationale de Football Association (FIFA) the international governing body of association football, responsible for the organisation of football's major international tournaments.

franchise an agreement whereby a particular club or sports star allows their name to be associated with a brand or product. The maker of the product pays for the right to use the club's name and in return receives the benefit of being associated with it.

human rights the basic rights and freedoms to which all humans are entitled, including the right to life, the right to liberty, and the right to work.

infrastructure physical structures, such as roads, railways and hospitals that underpin modern societies; can also extend to public services such as health, education and community sport.

international describes any activity or transaction between two or more countries.

less developed country (LDC) those countries that have a lower income, and poorer standards in health, nutrition, education and industry than more developed countries.

licensin an agreement in which a company, such as a sports goods manufacturer, can use the name or other aspects of a club or individual to promote its own products.

merchandise goods or products, often sold using the name of a particular club or sporting celebrity

more developed country (MDC) those countries that have a higher income, and better standards in health, nutrition, education and industry than less developed countries.

multiplier effect an effect which triggers further effects, rather like a chain reaction; for instance, the number of people directly involved in F1 racing is quite small, but the industry supports many other smaller businesses and manufacturers, so has a large (multiplier) effect on the economy and industry as a whole.

retail anything sold to the public rather than to other organisations or businesses.

revenue income, for example in relation to ticket sales, sponsorship or television deals between clubs and TV companies.

Soviet Union formerly a large part of western and mid-Asia, made up of Russia and a large number of surrounding territories, such as Georgia and Ukraine, which was broken up into individual countries in 1991.

sustainability the ability of any activity, particularly in environmental terms, to be maintained or developed without damaging future resources.

Union of European Football Associations (UEFA) the governing body of football in Europe, made up of national football associations.

United Nations (UN) a body formed by the majority of countries in the world, which seeks to bring about international agreements and co-operation in relation to issues such as international disputes, the environment and poverty.

United Nations Educational, Scientific and Cultural Organisation (UNESCO) An international body that encourages international peace and co-operation by promoting educational, scientific and cultural (including sporting) collaboration among nations.

Index